The Prom[illegible]

Ben Brown was born in London in [illegible] is plays include *Four Letter Word* (Edinburgh Fringe), Cameron Mackintosh New Writing Award 1994; *All Things Considered* (Stephen Joseph Theatre; Hampstead Theatre; Petit Théâtre de Paris; Marian Street Theatre, Sydney; Zimmertheater, Heidelberg), nominated for a Writers' Guild Best Play Award and the TMA Best New Play Award 1997; *Larkin With Women* (Stephen Joseph Theatre; West Yorkshire Playhouse; Coventry Belgrade; Manchester Library Theatre; Orange Tree Theatre 2006), Express Play of the Year, TMA Best New Play 2000.

by the same author

ALL THINGS CONSIDERED
LARKIN WITH WOMEN

BEN BROWN

The Promise

faber and faber

First published in 2010
by Faber and Faber Limited
74–77 Great Russell Street, London WC1B 3DA

Typeset by Country Setting, Kingsdown, Kent CT14 8ES
Printed in England by CPI Antony Rowe, Chippenham, Wiltshire

A CIP record for this book
is available from the British Library

ISBN 978–0–571–26887–0

2 4 6 8 10 9 7 5 3 1

For
Jessica and David

With love and thanks
to Jenny and my parents

The Promise was first presented on 17 February 2010 at the Orange Tree Theatre, London, with the following cast:

Chaim Weizmann Jonathan Tafler
Herbert Samuel Richard Clothier
Venetia Stanley Miranda Colchester
Herbert Asquith Christopher Ravenscroft
Edwin Montagu Nicholas Asbury
Arthur Balfour Oliver Ford Davies
Rabbi Joseph Sam Dastor
David Lloyd George Patrick Brennan
Alfred Milner Michael Sheldon
Max Beaverbrook Colin Stinton
Lord Curzon Sam Dastor
Abdullah Sam Dastor

Director Alan Strachan
Designer Sam Dowson
Lighting John Harris

Characters

Chaim Weizmann

Herbert Samuel

Venetia Stanley

Herbert Asquith

Edwin Montagu

Arthur Balfour

Rabbi Joseph

David Lloyd George

Alfred Milner

Max Beaverbrook

Lord Curzon

Abdullah

THE PROMISE

We lead dead men's lives.

Auguste Comte

ACT ONE

ONE	Samuel's office, 1914
TWO	Alderley Park, 1915
THREE	Balfour's home
FOUR	Montagu's home
FIVE	Cabinet Room
SIX	Cabinet Room
SEVEN	Lord Swaythling's house

ACT TWO

ONE	Montagu's home, 1917
TWO	Balfour's office
THREE	Montagu's home
FOUR	Cabinet Room
FIVE	Montagu's home
SIX	London Opera House
SEVEN	Government House, Jerusalem, 1925

Act One

ONE

As the house lights come down and the audience settles, the sound fades up on a contemporary news report relating to the Israel–Palestine conflict. The report is replaced by another. Then another and another, covering a range of events but all relating to Israel–Palestine.

Eventually, the sound fades out and the lights come up on a ministerial room in Whitehall, London. It is 10 December 1914.

Chaim Weizmann, forty and balding with a moustache and goatee beard and wearing a suit, sits nervously in a chair, sideways on to the audience.

Facing him is a large desk and behind that an empty chair.

Pause.

He looks at his watch.

Then continues waiting anxiously.

He gets up and wanders round the room.

He catches sight of himself in the mirror over the mantelpiece and goes over to it.

He checks his appearance in the mirror. Then smoothes his hair down.

Suddenly, the door opens and Herbert Samuel enters. He is forty-four and has thick wavy hair and a neatly trimmed moustache.

Weizmann, who speaks with a Russian accent, swings round to meet him.

Samuel Dr Weizmann.

Weizmann Yes.

Samuel Herbert Samuel.

He advances with an outstretched hand.
Weizmann shakes it.

Samuel Sorry you've had to wait. Today's Cabinet lasted a little longer than usual. Do sit down.

Weizmann Thank you.

He sits down as Samuel closes the door before returning to his seat.

Samuel So. What can I do for you?

Weizmann Well, if you don't mind, I'd rather wait for Mr Lloyd George before I begin. (*He looks at his watch.*) What time do you expect him?

Samuel Ah, yes, um . . . actually, I'm afraid the Chancellor can't make it this afternoon after all.

Weizmann (*hugely disappointed*) Oh . . .

Samuel Yes, the Prime Minister needed him at short notice on some urgent war business.

Weizmann I see. (*Abruptly getting up.*) Very well. I needn't detain you any longer then. I'll arrange to see him some other time.

He moves towards the door.

Samuel Wait a minute. You don't have to go. *I'm* still here.

He smiles.

Weizmann Yes, but I think it would be better to wait till Mr Lloyd George is present. I gather that he is especially interested in my cause.

Samuel And how do you know I'm not?

Weizmann hesitates.

Weizmann Look, to be frank Mr Samuel, it is the Chancellor I particularly wanted to see. I only came here because I was assured he would be present. Indeed, I would have preferred to see him alone, but I understand he requested your presence.

Samuel (*taken aback*) Well, thank you for your honesty. But I still don't understand why you won't talk to me.

Weizmann thinks.

Weizmann Well, let's just say that in my experience, men of your . . . type are not sympathetic to my point of view.

Samuel And what type is that?

Weizmann smiles.

Weizmann Mr Samuel, you are a rich, English Jew and have always been so. A member of the British Cabinet – the first practising Jew I believe ever to reach that position. So, you have no need to support radical causes. No reason to 'rock the boat' . . . I, on the other hand, am a poor Russian Jew, from a small town in the Pale of Settlement, which the Russian Government so kindly reserves for its six million Jews. Or at least I was until I came to England. I represent people who have nothing to lose. So, you see, we have little in common. Besides our . . .

Samuel Religion?

Weizmann It is more than that.

Samuel How so?

Weizmann hesitates.

Since you're here, you might as well say what you have to say.

Beat.

Weizmann Very well.

He pauses.

Consider for a moment . . . if you will . . . the history of our people over the last two thousand years.

Samuel raises his eyebrows.

Now it is, is it not, primarily a history of persecution and expulsion?

Samuel cannot deny it.

Since the Romans drove us out of Palestine, we have been expelled from England, France, Spain, Portugal, Austria, Hungary, Bavaria, Silesia, the Crimea . . . I could go on.

Samuel But that was hundreds of years ago.

Weizmann True, and I admit that in the West at least, matters have improved somewhat. But in the East – in Russia, Poland, Romania – well . . . the last thirty years have been the worst.

Pause.

Samuel So, what do you suggest?

Weizmann To me, it is obvious. We must return to our homeland, in Palestine. It was in Palestine that we lived as a nation and produced the highest fruits of our genius. Palestine alone, of all the countries on which the Jew has set foot, has an abiding place in his heart. So it is in Palestine that we must build our future.

He pauses.

Now, obviously, there is a problem in that Palestine is currently ruled by Turkey. But if only Britain was to help us, then that problem could easily be overcome.

Samuel smiles.

Samuel Yes, well –

Weizmann (*interrupting*) Please, before you dismiss the idea, let me finish. Because I would like to tell you how far we have already come. These last thirty years, since the pogroms started, thousands of Russian and Romanian Jews have gone to Palestine, despite all the difficulties the Turks put in our way. We have created settlements, where we grow grapes and oranges, olives and sesame. We have built schools and are bringing the Hebrew language back to life. And before the war began, I myself secured the backing of Baron Edmond de Rothschild for a Hebrew University in Jerusalem.

Samuel Really?

Weizmann Yes. Now, of course, the war has interrupted everything. But as soon as we can, we shall go on with our work, bringing more and more people in, buying more and more land, building up the Jewish community, bit by bit, step by step, until eventually, however long it takes, whatever obstacles are put in our way, the Jews shall once again live as a nation in Palestine.

Samuel smiles.

But no doubt you regard all this as a dream and a fantasy.

Samuel hesitates.

Samuel As a matter of fact . . . I don't.

Weizmann is surprised.

Though I have never spoken of it publicly, I have always had great sympathy with the Zionist cause. And now Turkey has allied herself with Germany, well . . . I think it may at last be possible to make the dream come true.

He smiles.
Weizmann smiles back at him in disbelief.
The lights fade.

TWO

The garden of Alderley Park in Cheshire, the country home of Lord Stanley. It is a warm spring morning.

Venetia Stanley, twenty-seven and good-looking in a dark, thoughtful way, sits on a bench working on a piece of embroidery depicting a tropical scene with animals and palm trees.

She seems agitated about something as she works away at the embroidery.

She pricks herself with the needle.

Venetia Damn.

She looks at her finger.

Then sucks it before continuing.

Pause.

Herbert Henry Asquith (sixty-two), a shortish, stocky-ish man with grey hair, enters and stops.

Asquith Ah, here you are . . .

He looks at her adoringly.

Venetia looks up.

Venetia Prime Minister.

Asquith No, don't move. You look so perfect just sitting there with your tapestry. It's at moments like this when I know why we're fighting this war.

Venetia smiles, without being taken in.

Venetia Is Margot here?

Asquith Yes. But I left her with your mother.

Venetia Ah . . .

Asquith I couldn't wait to see you.

He keeps looking at her.
She feels uneasy.

Venetia Yes, well . . . I'll get you some coffee.

She begins to get up.

Asquith No, please, stay where you are. I'd rather just sit here with you.

Venetia hesitates for a moment.

Venetia Very well.

She sits back down. Asquith sits down beside her and watches her as she does her embroidery.

Asquith It's going to be just us this weekend, isn't it? Besides your parents, I mean.

Venetia No, actually. I've invited Edwin too.

Asquith (*annoyed*) I thought he was going to Passover at his mother's?

Venetia Yes, well, he only stays for the Friday night. He's coming on this morning.

Asquith Oh, Venetia, must you invite him to everything? You see far too much of him in London as it is. Remember that poem I wrote for you.

Venetia, though a Christian child,
Sprung from an Aryan stem,
Frequents, too easily beguiled,
The silken tent of Shem.

He looks at her.

Venetia I like Edwin.

Asquith Oh, I like him. Very much. He's my most loyal colleague. My most devoted servant. But I'd rather be alone with you.

Venetia Well, you'd better make the most of it now then, hadn't you?

He smiles.

Asquith Quite right.

She continues doing her embroidery.

Now, put that aside for a moment please, and let me look at your hands.

She does so unenthusiastically and he takes her hands in his.

Ah, they are worth more than a king's ransom to me.

He looks concerned.

But what's this?

Venetia I just pricked my finger.

Asquith Oh . . . Still, no sign of your work at that horrible hospital yet, thank God.

Venetia (*gently removing her hands*) I've only been there a week.

Asquith I still don't understand why you have to go there at all. I hate the thought of you ministering to those diseased wastrels.

Venetia I don't have to. I want to.

Asquith Yes, that's the trouble. You are so good. Your sense of duty impels you. You want to relieve distress, don't you? Do your bit.

Venetia No, actually. I just thought it would be more interesting when a war's going on working in a hospital in the East End than spending all my time in a country house in Cheshire.

Asquith Nonsense. That's just your minimising way of talking.

Venetia No, it isn't. I'm not at all as you think I am, you know. I'm not a bit good. I'm not trying to improve myself morally. I just follow my inclination and interest.

Asquith smiles at her uncertainly.

Asquith I confess, I still don't understand you fully. Perhaps that's why I find you so fascinating.

Venetia returns wearily to her embroidery.

Venetia Anyway, tell me what you've been up to. I love to know what's going on in the war and the papers never tell me.

Asquith I should hope not, if the censors are doing their job properly. But I know I can trust you. You have never let me down.

He looks at her but she avoids his eyes.

So, I will tell you our most secret news.

Venetia stops doing her embroidery and looks at him.

We've decided to open another theatre.

Venetia is fascinated.

Venetia Really?

Asquith Well, what with the stalemate on the Western Front, we have to do something.

She thinks.

Venetia Where?

Asquith Well, we had a choice between Lloyd George's idea of landing a hundred thousand men in Syria to cut off the Turks retreating from Egypt, and Winston's idea of trying to force the Dardanelles to help Russia. Anyway, Kitchener prefers Winston's as it's a solely naval attack and therefore won't cost us so much in terms of ammunition and men. So we're going with that.

Venetia I see. How's Lloyd George taken it?

Asquith Not well. And I confess Admiral Fisher has his doubts too, but Winston says that if the naval bombardment alone is insufficient we can always land a small force at Gallipoli to finish the job. After which, with Russia properly supplied, the war could be over within three months.

Venetia considers this.

Venetia It seems worth the risk then, doesn't it?

Asquith I hope so . . . Oh, what a wise counsellor you are. I feel much better about it now I've spoken to you.

She can't help but smile.

You know, I was thinking this morning, it's now exactly three years since I made my discovery of the real you. Do you remember? We were sitting in the dining room of that house I'd been lent on the edge of the New Forest – just after you and Violet and Montagu and I had come back from Sicily – and we were talking and laughing, just the two of us, on our old accustomed terms, you being no more to me than my daughter's friend. And then suddenly, in a single instant, the scales dropped from my eyes, your features and smile and gestures assumed an absolutely new perspective and I knew that I had come to a turning point in my life. And so it has proved.

He looks at her.

And since this war began . . . well, my life would be intolerable without you.

Venetia avoids his eyes.

Promise me you'll never marry.

Venetia hesitates.

Venetia Why? It would make no difference to my feelings for you.

Asquith But it would devastate me.

Venetia is troubled.

Venetia Why?

Asquith Because it would ruin everything. Don't you see? I would no longer be able to confide in you all my greatest hopes and fears, all the most secret of state secrets. That deep confidence and trust that exists between us would immediately be broken and I'd be left without comfort and support, unable to cope.

Venetia But I'm twenty-seven. I shall have to marry some time.

Asquith Then at least wait till I'm dead.

Venetia I might be dead by then too, or too old.

Asquith Nonsense, I can't be long for this world, not with the strain I'm under . . .

He reflects.
Venetia looks at him with concern.
He sees her and perks up.

But then, when I'm gone, I want you to marry the most wonderful man in the world. So that if, like Moses, I may not enter the Promised Land, but only see it from afar, I can still think of it always, with its milk and honey and grapes and the rest – which I am not allowed to touch – as possessed and enjoyed by someone worthier than I could ever hope to be.

He smiles and takes her hand again.

At this moment, Edwin Montagu wanders towards them, wary of interrupting. He is thirty-six but looks older, prematurely balding, slightly untidy with a moustache less well trimmed than his cousin Herbert Samuel's and wearing a monocle in his left eye.

Venetia sees him first and withdraws her hand from Asquith.

Venetia Hello, Edwin.

Montagu Venetia.

Asquith Ah, Montagu.

Montagu Prime Minister.

A little pause.

Venetia How was Passover?

Montagu Well . . . it's over. What more can I say?

They smile.

But Prime Minister, I must talk to you urgently. In private.

Asquith Nonsense. Venetia and I have no secrets from each other, do we, Venetia?

Venetia smiles uncomfortably and glances at Montagu.

Montagu Very well. (*Beat.*) It's being said that the attacks on you in *The Times* are part of Northcliffe's campaign to supplant you with Lloyd George, who will then form a coalition with Balfour as Foreign Secretary.

Asquith takes it in.

Asquith Yes, so I've heard.

Montagu You've heard?

Asquith Yes. And I've spoken to Lloyd George about it.

Edwin and Venetia are surprised.

Montagu What did he say?

Asquith He denied it. Indeed, he said he owed me everything and would rather break stones, dig potatoes or be hanged and quartered than be disloyal to me.

Montagu And you believe him?

Asquith Certainly. And as for what *The Times* has been saying, he says Kitchener is the real culprit because, in spite of every warning, he has neglected up to the eleventh hour a proper provision of munitions – but as he's a Tory, or supposed to be, *The Times* is reluctant to attack him and so is attacking me instead. All of which I find far more plausible than these rumours that Lloyd George is conspiring with that snake Balfour.

Montagu Well, I hope you're right.

Asquith Of course I'm right. That's why I'm Prime Minister.

He smiles at Venetia.

(*To Montagu.*) Oh, by the way, I've just had the most extraordinary memorandum from your cousin.

Montagu Oh yes, what about?

Asquith Palestine.

Montagu is surprised.

Montagu Palestine?

Asquith Yes, and Zionism. Didn't you get a copy?

Montagu No.

Asquith Oh, that's odd. Well, I dare say you will.

Montagu looks troubled.

Anyway, I'd better go and say hello to Venetia's parents or they'll think I only come here to admire their daughter.

Asquith smiles at Venetia and goes.
Montagu watches him go, thoughtfully.

Venetia What's Zionism?

Montagu A movement to return the Jews to Palestine. Mount Zion is in Jerusalem.

Venetia Oh. (*She thinks.*) How interesting . . .

Montagu Ludicrous more like. You can't turn the clock back eighteen hundred years.

Venetia Eighteen hundred years?

Montagu That's when the Romans kicked us out.

Venetia Ah . . . Yes, now I come to think of it, in the Bible you all seemed to be there . . . and now you're everywhere.

Montagu Quite. (*Beat.*) But we have more important things to discuss than cousin Herbert's memorandum.

He takes her hands in his.

I take it you haven't told him yet?

Venetia (*moving away from him*) No. I was going to but then he suddenly seemed so especially vulnerable today.

Montagu And he has no idea?

Venetia No, I don't think it's occurred to him that I would ever marry you.

Montagu . . . Because I'm Jewish?

She considers this.

Venetia Yes, I suppose it is really.

Montagu takes this in.

Montagu How do you think he'll take it?

Venetia Badly. He's told me again and again that if I were to marry life would have nothing left to offer him. How could he say that to me? He has no claim on me. The man's married, for God's sake. Besides being old enough to be my father.

Montagu Yes, well, that is the conventional view.

She reflects.

Venetia Oh, if only I'd accepted you three years ago when you first asked me, then it wouldn't really have mattered to him. He would soon have found someone else who would have done just as well as me. But now . . . Oh, what a fool I've been to have let it get to this.

Montagu looks concerned.

Montagu Perhaps you should try and gradually detach yourself from him first?

Venetia No, I've thought of that, but it would be impossible. I might manage not to see him for a week or so and make excuses for not doing so but then there'd be a scene and in order to mollify him I'd say anything he wanted.

She frowns.

Oh, why can't I make you both happy?

Montagu That's not the way life works.

Venetia No . . .

Montagu And besides, I want you all to myself.

He takes her hands again. Venetia looks uncomfortable.

Venetia Do you?

Montagu Of course.

Venetia Even if I don't have the feelings for you that a wife is supposed to have?

Montagu is depressed for a moment.

Montagu Yes. I've told you, you needn't worry about that. Women often feel that way before they're married, don't they? And in the meantime we can still be very happy together.

Venetia . . . I hope so.

Montagu Of course we can.

He smiles.

But first you have to tell the PM.

Venetia Yes . . .

Montagu Or do you want me to do it?

Venetia No. It'll be better coming from me. I'll tell him soon, I promise.

He nods and smiles.

Now, come on, we'd better go and join the others. It's almost time for lunch.

She picks up her embroidery.

Montagu Very well, but we must find a time to discuss your conversion, unless you want me to be disinherited.

Venetia No, I don't want that . . . But, please, one problem at a time . . .

They go off.

THREE

4 Carlton Gardens, the home of Arthur Balfour, Tory ex-Prime Minister.

Balfour (sixty-six), tall and urbane, with thinning grey hair and a moustache, stands, informally dressed, facing a suited, seated Weizmann.

Balfour Yes, I remember. I was fighting for my seat in the 1906 election, which is no doubt why I agreed to see you. I was rather unpopular with the Jews at the time since I'd just brought in the Aliens Act. And you were said to be a well-known Manchester Zionist . . . But it didn't make any difference. I still lost my seat.

Weizmann Not because of me, Mr Balfour, I assure you.

Balfour smiles.

Balfour Do you still live in Manchester?

Weizmann Yes.

Balfour Married?

Weizmann Yes, with two sons. My wife is a doctor. Also from Russia. She works in the maternity ward at Victoria Hospital.

Balfour Ah . . . And you're still teaching at the University?

Weizmann Yes. And I have my research of course . . .

Balfour Oh yes, what's that about?

Weizmann hesitates.

Weizmann Well, there's an element of secrecy about it . . . but I'm sure it's all right to tell you. Right now I am working for the Government to try and find a way of producing more acetone.

Balfour thinks.

Balfour Acetone . . . ?

Weizmann It's the solvent in making cordite for our shells. We have a shortage.

Balfour Ah, yes. Important work then . . .

Weizmann Yes.

Balfour is impressed.

Balfour Anyway, what did you wish to discuss with me?

Weizmann Well, last time, you may remember, I explained to you why we Zionists rejected your kind offer of a homeland in Uganda.

Balfour Yes . . .

Weizmann Well, now I would like to tell you what this war means for my people and why it is more important than ever to find a lasting solution. You see, they do not write about it in the papers, but right now, in Poland, Jews are being attacked and killed on an unprecedented scale. Vilna, Grodno, Byelostok – all have witnessed terrible pogroms carried out, I regret to say, under the authority of our Russian allies. And when I talk about pogroms I know what I'm saying . . . Eleven years ago I happened to be in Russia in the town of Kishinev when the Jewish quarter was attacked. We defended ourselves as best we could, but I saw men murdered, homes and businesses destroyed, women and girls dragged away screaming . . . Well, the reports I am getting now from Poland make that seem like child's play.

Balfour nods sympathetically.

Balfour Yes, well, war is a terrible thing . . .

He reflects for a moment, then recovers.

But to look to the future, my current view is that the Jews will never be totally secure until they either become entirely assimilated – and, by that, I mean, intermarriage – or until they find a home of their own. And if, as you say, they won't accept anywhere else, I suppose that must be in Palestine. Personally, I think it a shame the Jews are so against intermarriage as they are a most gifted race and it would be to our advantage as well as theirs if they were to assimilate in every way.

Weizmann But that would mean the end of the Jews and Judaism. And you don't want that, do you?

Balfour Well, no, of course not, but –

Weizmann I mean, we don't want the world to become like a library with numerous copies of the same book, do we?

Balfour smiles.
Then hesitates.

Balfour Let me tell you something that might interest you . . . About a year or two ago, on a trip to Bayreuth, I had a long talk about the Jewish Question with Cosima Wagner.

Weizmann is surprised.

Weizmann Really?

Balfour Yes. And to tell you the truth, I couldn't help agreeing with much of what she said. You see, the way she sees it –

Weizmann holds up his hand.

Weizmann Please. I spent some time in Germany and I know how the argument goes. Let *me* tell *you* what she said.

Balfour smiles.

Balfour Very well.

Weizmann thinks.

Weizmann Mrs Wagner thinks that the Jews in Germany have captured the stage, the press, commerce, the universities, etc., and that they are putting into their pockets, after only a hundred years of emancipation, everything for which Germans have worked for centuries, and that she, Mrs Wagner, and people who think like her, resent very much having to receive all their moral and material culture at their hands.

Balfour (*impressed*) Yes. That was the gist of it.

Weizmann Well, this may surprise you, but I too agree with her.

Balfour (*surprised*) You do?

Weizmann Certainly. As to the facts. But I totally disagree as to the conclusions to be drawn. After all, these Jews have assimilated as much as they can, taken a great part in building up Germany – as other Jews have helped build up France and England – at the expense of the Jewish people as a whole, whose sufferings increase with the absorption of their most creative elements into their surrounding communities – who then reproach us for this absorption and react with anti-Semitism. But the real tragedy is that whereas we do not recognise these Jewish grandees as Jews, Madame Wagner does not recognise them as Germans. And so we stand as the most exploited and misunderstood of peoples.

Balfour nods with understanding.

So, you see, assimilation is not the answer. It has gone further in Germany than anywhere and it is not working. The Jews are still not accepted. On the other hand, a home other than Palestine will never be acceptable to Jews.

And they will certainly never produce either the money or the energy required to build up a wasteland and make it habitable unless that land is Palestine. So a home in Palestine is the only way. There we will create what I like to call the hundred-per-cent Jew. Instead of the assimilated Jew of the West and the oppressed Jew of the East, we shall see a new Jew, settled in his own land, speaking his own language, living amongst his own people and leading a normal Jewish life for the first time in eighteen hundred years.

Balfour takes it in.

Balfour I see . . . A noble dream. But how are you to get hold of Palestine in the first place?

Weizmann Well, you will have seen that Mr Asquith has declared his intention to dismember the Turkish Empire.

Balfour Of course.

Weizmann So, we see this war, appalling as it is, as our golden opportunity. Britain occupies Palestine . . . then we move in. At least, that is what I am working on with Mr Samuel.

Balfour is surprised.

Balfour Herbert Samuel?

Weizmann Yes.

Balfour Then you have a man on the inside . . .

Weizmann Yes.

Balfour thinks.

Balfour (*decisively*) Very well. I will also help you. If I can. But my party is not in power. So what do you want me to do?

Weizmann Nothing.

Balfour Nothing?

Weizmann Not as long as the guns are roaring. All I wanted was to explain to you how wide and deep is the bloodstained tragedy of my people and to convince you that our salvation, with Britain's help, could soon be within our grasp.

Balfour Well, you've done that most eloquently.

Weizmann Thank you. But I'd like to call on you again, with your permission, when the military situation has become clearer.

Balfour Of course.

Weizmann That is all I ask. (*Getting up.*) Now I need not take up any more of your weekend.

Balfour gets up and takes his hand.

Balfour Mind you do come again. I am deeply interested . . . It is not a dream. It is a great cause and I understand it.

Weizmann is thrilled.

Weizmann Thank you.

They smile.
Then Weizmann goes, leaving Balfour alone to reflect.

FOUR

Montagu's handsome home at 24 Queen Anne's Gate, Kensington.
Montagu and Venetia wait anxiously in the drawing room.
A tense silence.

Venetia I hope this is really necessary.

Montagu It is. I've checked with my solicitor and there's no way round it. My father's will is quite clear. If I marry someone not of the Jewish faith, I lose my inheritance. Ten thousand pounds a year, upon which I am totally dependent. No more Rolls Royces or (*looking around the opulent room*) houses in Queen Anne's Gate . . . So I know it's absurd, and I regard it as as wrong to have to look for a wife according to her religion as I would according to the colour of her eyes, but unless you want to be poor, there is really no alternative.

Venetia thinks.

Venetia Well . . . I must admit, I think on the whole people are happier rich than poor . . . but God knows what my father will say . . .

Montagu Why, is he very religious?

Venetia No. He's an atheist.

Montagu is surprised.

Still, one of his brothers became a Muslim and another a Roman Catholic priest, so I dare say he'll get over it eventually.

Montagu smiles.

Isn't it depressing, though, that among all our friends and relations there isn't one who will be anything other than annoyed by our marriage?

Montagu My family won't be. Once you've come in, that is. They'll be delighted.

Venetia (*surprised*) You mean, you've told them?

Montagu Well . . . only my mother and brother and sister. I had to really, once I'd told Rabbi Joseph.

Venetia shrugs.

Venetia Yes, well, 'coming in', as you put it, is precisely what will upset my family most.

She reflects.
Then looks at her watch.

Was it really necessary to meet him? Couldn't I have satisfied him in writing?

Montagu No. You can't become a Jew by post you know.

Venetia . . . No, I suppose not.

Montagu And he is the most accommodating Rabbi in London. Indeed, he was forced out of cousin Herbert's synagogue for being too liberal.

Venetia Why, what did he do?

Montagu Oh, I don't know. Let men and women sit together, or prayed in English rather than Hebrew or something. Anyway, he's agreed to do you with the minimum of fuss, so we must be grateful to him . . . By the way, did you get a chance to read that book of his I gave you?

Venetia I tried but it was just too boring. *Judaism as Creed and Life* – not my cup of tea really.

Montagu frowns.

Montagu Look, just try and think of it as an examination. You needn't actually believe it. God knows, I don't.

He drinks.
The sound of the doorbell.
They look at each other.
Then Montagu goes out.
Venetia waits nervously during the following.

Rabbi Joseph (*off, to the butler*) I have an appointment with Mr Montagu and Miss Stanley.

Montagu (*off*) Hello, Rabbi Joseph.

Rabbi Joseph (*off*) Ah, Edwin. So nice to see you. It's been too long . . .

Montagu (*off*) Yes, well, do come through.

Rabbi Joseph (*off*) Thank you.

Rabbi Joseph (sixty-six), with a grey beard and wearing a dog collar, comes into the drawing room followed by Montagu.

Montagu Venetia, this is Rabbi Joseph. Rabbi Joseph, Miss Stanley.

Venetia How do you do.

Rabbi Joseph Delighted to meet you, Miss Stanley.

He goes over and takes her hand. Venetia smiles politely.

And congratulations on your engagement.

Venetia Thank you.

Pause.

Montagu Can I offer you some refreshment, Rabbi?

Rabbi Joseph Not just yet, thank you. But perhaps after Miss Stanley and I have had our little talk . . .

Montagu Of course. Well . . . I'll leave you to it then.

He exchanges a little look with Venetia before slipping out of the room.

Rabbi Joseph waits for Venetia to sit down before sitting opposite her.

Then smiles kindly at her.

Rabbi Joseph Now firstly, I just want to say what a privilege it is to initiate you into our faith.

Venetia Yes, well . . . it's very good of you to take me on.

Rabbi Joseph Not at all. Anyway, I gather Mr Montagu's already given you my book . . .

Venetia Yes . . .

Rabbi Joseph Well, I don't know how far you've got . . .

Venetia Well, not very, actually . . .

Rabbi Joseph (*disappointed*) Oh. Well, never mind. In any case, I propose to just jump in at the deep end, as it were.

He smiles.

Now, the good news is that I always think it's easier to convert to Judaism from Christianity than from, well, anything else, so to speak. You see, both share a belief in what Christians call the Old Testament and we call the Torah, and both accept the concept of monotheism, or, as I like to put it, the Unity of the Divine.

Venetia Yes . . .

Rabbi Joseph That is Judaism's great gift to the world . . . But here is where we come to the real issue at stake. Because if there is only one God, how can we at the same time say that God is three?

Venetia hesitates.

Venetia Mm . . .

Rabbi Joseph You see, it doesn't really make sense, does it? Isn't it far easier to stick with the idea of One God without saying God is also three, or three in one, or one in three, or anything like that?

Venetia thinks.

Venetia Yes, I see what you mean.

Rabbi Joseph Do you? Excellent. Then you are well on the way already.

He beams at Venetia, who smiles back uncomfortably.

And that's about all there is to it really in the way of theological belief. Easy, isn't it?

Venetia nods.

Venetia Mm . . .

Rabbi Joseph Good. Well, let's move on to the observances then, shall we? Now, these fall into two main categories, our dietary laws and our holy days. So, to begin with the holy days . . .

The lights begin to fade as Venetia tries to look interested.

These are, besides the Sabbath, of course, the three joyous festivals: Passover, Pentecost, and the Tabernacles; the two solemn celebrations: New Year and the Day of Atonement; the two minor feasts: Chanukah and Purim; and the historic Fast of the Ninth of Ab . . .

The lights fade to black.

Fade up some time later.
Venetia drinks from a wine glass.
Montagu comes into the room and looks at her.

Montagu So?

Venetia thinks.

Venetia Well, I think I managed to pull the wool . . . Though I did get a little confused about the Paschal lamb . . .

Montagu smiles.

But what a farce! Were I to be washed a thousand times in the waters of the Jordan and go through every rite and ceremony the strictest Jewish creed involved, I should not feel I had changed my race or religion one iota.

Montagu Fine. I'm not asking you to.

Venetia Aren't you?

Montagu No, this is just because of my father's will, remember?

But she is still concerned.

Venetia So you won't expect me to do anything afterwards?

Montagu No, of course not.

Venetia I'll still be able to eat pork and lobster?

Montagu smiles

Montagu Of course.

Venetia smiles.
Pause.
Montagu thinks.

Look, when this is over, all I will ever ask of you is the avowal, if challenged, that you have thrown in your lot with us. That if we are attacked or scorned, you count yourself as one of us. And that honestly is the only time I find one ever thinks of it.

Venetia thinks.

Venetia But what about our children? Old Joseph seems pretty keen that we should bring them up as Jews.

Montagu Yes, well, personally I have always thought that no religious teaching was the right thing and mean to stick to that. Indeed, I think it would be unloving to try and influence them in any way.

Venetia But what about when they ask what religion we are?

Montagu Well, then they shall be told that their father was born a Jew and remained one throughout his life, that their mother was a Jew by adoption, and that they were therefore born Jews. But if they want a religion to practise, though you and I practise none, they can choose their own. And if when they're grown up they want to marry Christians, Hindus or Muslims, they will have no criticism from me, nor shall I think any the worse of them.

He looks at her.

But I admit this. If they choose to marry in – which I do not think likely given the circles we move in – but if they do, I shall be pleased.

Venetia is surprised.

Venetia Really? How interesting . . .

She thinks.

But no . . . I don't think it likely either.

She drinks.
Pause.

Montagu Anyway, he told me you'd soon be ready to take the plunge.

Venetia Not literally, I hope. I've told you I don't want the full immersion.

Montagu No, no, don't worry. I'm sure we can get round that. Though, believe me, there's a much tougher requirement for men.

Venetia smiles.

Montagu He said you just need to make a sincere declaration of faith, that's all.

Venetia Or appear to, you mean.

Montagu Yes. But you must take it seriously, or appear to, or you'll find that not even the daughter of Lord Stanley is so irresistible that they are prepared to be made fools of.

Venetia Don't worry, I'll do my bit.

Montagu I know you will.

They smile.

So, that just leaves the matter of the PM . . .

Venetia Yes . . .

Montagu You still haven't told him?

Venetia No. I keep meaning to and then something crops up in the war and I can't face it. What with this Dardanelles business and the shell fiasco, it just seems cruel to hit a man when he's down. And he seems to be getting more and more dependent on me. He writes to me every day and was very upset I couldn't dine with him this evening. Margot's in the country.

Montagu What excuse did you make?

Venetia Well, I couldn't very well tell him I was coming here to practise for my conversion, could I? It would have rather given the game away.

Montagu All the better. So what did you say?

Venetia I told him I had a bandaging class.

Montagu shakes his head.

Montagu The longer it goes on the harder it will be.

Venetia I know. I'll tell him soon, I promise.

Montagu You've said that before.

Venetia I know. But it seems so much more real now.

She finishes her drink and puts the glass down.

Come on. It's time you drove me back to the hospital.

Montagu Already?

Venetia I don't want to get locked out again.

Montagu sighs.

Montagu I can't wait till we're married.

They go off.

FIVE

The Cabinet Room at 10 Downing Street.

The small five-man War Cabinet sit round a table as Lloyd George (fifty-one) – Chancellor of the Exchequer, and immediately recognisable from his Welsh accent – speaks to them in full flow.

Samuel, Montagu and Milner (a quiet, efficient man of sixty) listen.

Asquith, however, is absorbed in writing a letter, while taking care that his neighbours should not see what he is writing.

Lloyd George So as I've said time and time and again, we are never going to get our soldiers properly armed or make the elusive breakthrough on the Western Front if the Secretary of State for War insists on keeping responsibility for the supply and delivery of munitions in his own hands. He has more than enough on his plate as it is, which is no doubt why he can't even find the time to be here today, let alone solve the shell crisis. And now the Army is engaged in Gallipoli too, trying to pull the Navy's chestnuts out of the fire, as I warned it would, it's even more vital we sort this mess out. And the solution, if only the Secretary of State for War could see it, or be made to see it, is staring us in the face. What we need is a Ministry of Munitions. Kitchener can then simply say what the Army needs in terms of shells and bullets and so forth, while someone else, with experience of civil affairs, is given the responsibility of actually ordering and delivering the damn things. After which, the Army, properly supplied at last, might finally be able to make some progress towards winning this bloody war.

Milner and Samuel nod and 'Mm' their agreement.
Montagu is suspicious.
Lloyd George looks to the Prime Minister for his reaction but Asquith continues writing his letter.

Lloyd George Prime Minister?

Asquith stops writing and looks up.

Asquith Hm?

Lloyd George What do you think of my proposal?

Asquith Sorry, I missed that last bit. What were you saying exactly?

Lloyd George takes a deep breath, barely able to hide his frustration.

Lloyd George I was saying we need to set up a new Ministry of Munitions, separate from the War Ministry and with sole responsibility for supply, if we are ever to solve our shell shortage.

Asquith Yes, well, you know how the Secretary of State for War feels about that. And he assures me that he and the First Lord of the Admiralty are solving these problems themselves even as we speak, so I don't see there's much more we can usefully do for the moment. We must place our trust in their wisdom. Wait and see if matters improve.

Lloyd George With all due respect, Prime Minister, in this matter, isn't it time we replaced 'wait and see' with a bit of push and go?

Asquith is surprised at the obvious dig.
The others wait for a reaction.

Asquith I'll keep your suggestion in mind. Now, what other business?

Lloyd George seethes as Milner looks through the agenda.

Milner Mr Samuel's Palestine proposal is the last item on the agenda.

Asquith Ah yes. Go ahead.

Samuel Thank you.

As Samuel speaks, Asquith finishes his letter.

Yes, well, following on from my memorandum, the question I wish to address – not too prematurely I hope – is, if the war results in the break-up of the Turkish Empire in Asia, what is to be the future of Palestine?

Expressions of interest. Asquith puts the letter in an envelope and puts it in his pocket.
Samuel gets up and pulls down a large map of the Middle East on the back wall facing the audience.
He picks up a stick and points to the relevant countries where necessary.

Now, of course, the possibility most frequently discussed is annexation by France, because of the strong position she already occupies in Syria and the Lebanon. However, it is clear that the presence of a great European Power so close to the Suez Canal would be a great danger to the British Empire since we cannot proceed on the supposition that our present happy relations with France will continue always.

Lloyd George (*approvingly*) Mm . . .

Samuel Another possibility is the establishment of some kind of international regime. But internationalisation has invariably proved a stepping-stone to something else and in this case it could be annexation by Germany. Germany has already been very active in Palestine and has spent considerable sums of money there with a view to increasing her influence. Needless to say, a German Palestine would be a grave threat both to England in Egypt and France in Northern Syria.

Nods from everyone but Montagu, who listens with concern.

The last alternative usually discussed is the establishment of an independent Jewish state . . .

He looks round.

However, whatever may be the merits or demerits of that proposal, the time is not ripe for it.

Montagu is puzzled.

If the attempt were made to place six hundred thousand Arabs under a Government which rested upon the support of the mere ninety thousand Jewish inhabitants, there can be no assurance that it would be able to command respect and obedience. And even if the state did succeed in avoiding or repressing internal disorder, it is doubtful whether it would be strong enough to protect itself from external aggression.

He pauses.

Having discarded the usual suggestions then, I should now like to propose my own solution, namely, a British Protectorate.

Palestine in British hands would be a safeguard to the Suez Canal, since although it would of course itself be open to attack, the mountainous character of the country would make its occupation by an enemy difficult, and, while this outpost was being contested, time would be given to allow Egypt's defences to be strengthened.

Lloyd George and Milner nod with interest.

Furthermore, it would enable England to forward the purpose for which, at bottom, her Empire exists. Under the Turk, Palestine has been blighted. For hundreds of years she has produced neither men nor things useful to the world. The present inhabitants are sunk in squalor. Corruption is universal. Should England assume control, what has been achieved in Egypt could be repeated in Palestine, and the knowledge of this would make many of the present inhabitants not merely acquiesce but rejoice in the change. Thus, by this means, England can fulfil in yet another sphere her historic role of civiliser of the backward countries.

He smiles.

Finally, I am assured, both by Zionists and non-Zionists, that a British Protectorate would be by far the most welcome solution to Jews throughout the world – provided, that is, Jewish organisations are allowed to purchase land, found colonies, establish educational institutions and generally forward the economic development of the country. Further, if Jewish immigration – carefully regulated, of course – were to be given preference, in the course of time the Jewish people, grown into a majority and settled in the land, might be granted such a degree of self-government as the conditions of that day may justify.

Montagu frowns.

Now, I admit that such an outcome will not solve the Jewish problem in Europe. A country the size of Wales, much of it barren mountain and part of it waterless, cannot hold nine million people. But it could in time hold three or four million and thus reduce the pressure in Russia. Let then a Jewish centre be established in Palestine, let it achieve, as I believe it would achieve, a spiritual and intellectual greatness, and insensibly, but inevitably, the character of the individual Jew, wherever he might be, will be enobled, the sordid associations which have attached to the Jewish name will be sloughed off, and the value of the Jews as an element in the civilisation of the European peoples will be enhanced.

He sits down.
Pause.

Lloyd George Yes, of course, the real problem is the French. They claim Palestine is merely southern Syria and should therefore come under their sphere of influence. But that's what I like so much about this proposal. Through the Jews we can save the Christian holy places from France.

Asquith Milner?

Milner Yes, well, as the Chancellor says, if we can get it past the French . . .

Asquith Montagu?

Montagu pauses for a moment and looks at the pages of notes he has been taking.
He smiles.

Montagu I take a different view . . . But if I may, I would like to deal with the President of the Local Government Board's suggestion point by point.

He stands up, goes to the map and picks up the stick, pointing to countries where necessary.

Firstly, I think it is quite clear that the position of Palestine in itself offers little or no attraction to Great Britain from a strategic point of view. It would not be a buffer between our vital route to India through the Suez Canal on the one hand, and French, Turkish or, God help us, German interests on the other, but on the contrary an exposed flank . . . Commercially too, Palestine, which contains no oil or mineral wealth, is an incomparably poorer possession than, say, Mesopotamia. So it seems to me that in truth the interest in the question is really confined to the possibility of ultimately founding a Jewish state there.

He looks at Samuel, who doesn't contradict him, then puts the stick down and returns to his seat as he continues.

Well, I have always understood that Jewish hopes of a return to the Promised Land are based on a particular interpretation of divine prophecy in the Old Testament and are to be achieved by divine leadership, but I have never heard it said, even by his most fervent admirers, that the President of the Local Government Board is the Messiah.

A ripple of amusement passes around the Cabinet.

In any case, I think it would indeed require nothing short of a miracle to produce a Jewish state in Palestine, or anywhere else for that matter, as the Jews today are a polyglot, many-coloured, heterogeneous collection of people of different civilisations and traditions, and the confusion generated by any attempt to form a Jewish state could not be any very great improvement on that which followed the erection of the Tower of Babel.

More smiles.

And as to the suggestion I have heard that Hebrew could be used as a common language, it could no more serve as a means of communication than Latin could for Roman Catholics. Hebrew to the vast majority of Jews is a language in which to pray but not a language in which to speak or write. Indeed, I doubt whether the President of the Local Government Board could translate a single sentence of his memorandum into Hebrew.

Samuel doesn't respond.

Besides, how would the Jews be expected to occupy themselves in Palestine? Agriculture is never attractive to ambitious people and the Jews in the main have long emerged into quicker, less pastoral pursuits. Certainly, I cannot see any Jews I know tending olive trees or herding sheep.

He looks at Samuel.

Or is my cousin to be asked to look after the Borough Council of Jerusalem rather than the West Riding of Yorkshire? The Lord Chief Justice to reside at the Beth Din instead of the Court of Appeal? And myself to appoint rabbis in the Duchy of Lebanon rather than Anglican parsons in the Duchy of Lancaster?

More smiles.

As for the effect on the Jewish problem in Russia and elsewhere, the President of the Local Government Board himself admits that Palestine could in time hold a maximum of only three million out of nine million downtrodden Eastern Jews. But what about the six million left behind? (*He looks around the room.*) I venture to predict that in those countries where anti-Semitism is at its maximum, the position of Jewish citizens, when they have a country of their own to which they can be invited to clear out, would be infinitely worse than it is at present.

He thinks.

To sum up, I regard what has been put before us today as a proposal that, though trimmed with rather thin arguments of strategy and foreign policy, is in reality a presumptuous and almost blasphemous attempt to forestall divine agency in the collection of the Jews, which would be punished, if not by a new captivity in Babylon, by a new and unrivalled persecution of those left behind.

Surprised at his vehemence, no one speaks for a moment.

Samuel May I ask then, if Britain is not to take control of Palestine and form a Protectorate for the Jews, what is to become of it? Let the French have it? Leave it with the Turk? Lay it under the dead hand of internationalisation and allow it to become a theatre of intrigue, before in time the Germans fill the vacuum?

Montagu thinks.

Montagu What about the Arabs?

Samuel The Arabs?

Montagu Yes. Haven't we already promised it to them anyway?

Asquith (*looking to Milner*) Have we?

Milner I believe the wording of the High Commissioner of Egypt's undertaking to the Sharif of Mecca is ambiguous as to whether Palestine is to be included in the territory of a future Arab state or not.

Montagu All right then. What about the people who live there?

Samuel You mean, the Palestinian Arabs who are currently fighting against us with their Turkish masters? Why should we reward our enemies?

Montagu Better that than damn the Jews.

Samuel It isn't damning them, it will be their salvation.

Montagu Ha.

Asquith (*stepping in*) Yes, well, fortunately, none of this need be decided now in any case. Palestine is not yet in our gift. But we can consider it together with the rest of our desiderata for the eventual peace settlement. Or in other words, yes, wait and see. It is often the best policy. (*He smiles at Lloyd George.*) Now, I think that's everything, isn't it?

Milner nods.

Asquith Good. Thank you, gentlemen.

They get up to leave.

Lloyd George Well, I enjoyed that anyway. I'd rather talk about Palestine than the Western Front any day.

Milner Yes, most interesting.

Lloyd George It has a grandeur and romance about it. Jerusalem, Bethlehem, the Mount of Olives . . . the names of the places are as familiar to me as the valleys of Wales . . .

Samuel, Lloyd George and Milner go, leaving Montagu and Asquith behind.

Montagu waits till they're out of earshot.

Montagu Prime Minister, you don't really believe Samuel's proposal is anything but ludicrous, do you?

Asquith smiles.

Asquith No, don't worry. I'm not in the least tempted by your cousin's wild ideas, whatever Lloyd George may think of them. It seems to me a highly improbable fantasy. And we have enough imperial responsibilities as it is. But it won't do any harm to humour them a little for now. Unity is important and we must let them down lightly.

Montagu smiles.

Montagu Forgive me. I should never have doubted you.

Venetia comes in through the open door. She is dressed for dinner.

(*Surprised.*) Venetia!

Asquith looks up in excitement and smiles.

Venetia Hello. Sorry to interrupt. I thought you'd finished.

Asquith Don't be silly. You can interrupt whenever you like, can't she, Edwin?

Montagu Of course.

Asquith Now, just wait here a moment and I'll be with you in one minute. I'm sure Mr Montagu will be happy to keep you company.

Asquith goes out.

Montagu What are you doing here?

Venetia I'm having dinner with him tonight.

Montagu But I thought you said you were busy this evening?

Venetia I am. This is my engagement.

Montagu is annoyed.

Montagu Well, can you dine with me tomorrow then?

Venetia I'll see. He asked me to keep it free. But we can have a drink at six thirty. He won't be back till seven.

Montagu smarts.

Montagu Oh, this is too much. I'm supposed to be your fiancé.

Venetia shrugs.

Venetia What can I do? He writes to me five times a day. He cancelled his weekly meeting with the King because the hospital gave me some time off. He says he can't do anything now without discussing it with me first.

Montagu But you promised me you'd tell him.

Venetia I know. And I will. Soon.

Montagu So you keep saying. But can you possibly expect me to go on being allowed to see you only when he is not free? I hoped for a gradual ending to this, but I can see you are becoming more an element in his life than ever. You drove yesterday, you dine today, you can't even let me know when I might see you till you see what he wants and I am allowed six thirty tomorrow because he won't be back till seven. Can a lover who means business put up with it?

Venetia says nothing.

Montagu Or perhaps you've changed your mind?

Venetia No . . . I haven't.

Montagu Well then. See it through. And if you won't do it for my sake, do it for your own . . . and his. I tell you, this relationship spells trouble for him. He's obsessed with you and it shows. He was writing to you in Cabinet again today.

Venetia They won't know it was me.

Montagu It's obvious it isn't work. Everyone can see that. Lloyd George was particularly irritated. And it's damaging him. We're fighting a war, you know, and the Prime Minister needs to have his mind on that, not on you.

Venetia takes this in.
Pause.

Venetia You're right. I'll tell him now.

He looks her in the eye.

Montagu Good. See that you do then.

He hesitates for a moment.

I'll see you tomorrow.

He goes, leaving Venetia alone to think.
She goes to the window and looks out.
Long pause.
Eventually, Asquith returns.

Asquith Right. Sorry about that. The Admiralty wanted to talk about this Dardanelles business.

She nods.

Where's Montagu?

Venetia Oh . . . he had to go.

Asquith Really? How unlike him to leave you alone. But I can't say I'm sorry . . .

He smiles and holds out a hand.

Now, come and sit down with me for a moment.

Reluctantly, she does so.
He takes her hand.

Asquith Ah, these hands . . .

He strokes them but stops as he sees something.

But what's this?

Venetia Nothing. Just a slight swelling.

Asquith They're chilblains.

Venetia Well, perhaps.

Asquith But that's terrible. It's that dreadful hospital. It must be affecting your circulation.

Venetia Really, I'm fine.

Asquith Well, you must get them looked at.

Venetia I have. And they're not serious.

Asquith Good. Because you must keep yourself well. And especially your dear hands. I depend on them you know, and as the country depends on me, the country depends on them too.

She can't help but smile.

Seriously though, I often think in these trying times it's only you that keeps me going. The latest Dardanelles casualties include some young men I knew. Wilding, the lawn tennis champion . . . Rupert Brooke . . .

Venetia takes it in.

Why should people like myself be allowed to linger on the stage, when so much vividness and promise is cut short?

He reflects.

Perhaps Northcliffe and his obscene crew at *The Times* are right – whatever the rest of the world may say. I am, if not an impostor, at any rate a failure and ultimately a fool . . . I suppose most people would say that I had got at least a fair share of what men desire and struggle for and aim at in life. But 'what shall it profit a man to gain the whole world and lose his own soul?' For 'my own soul' is not wholly, or wholeheartedly, engaged in the things that seem, and probably are, of supreme importance.

He looks at her.

The truth is, I care more about you than anything else. Including this wretched war.

He reaches for her hands again, but she pulls them away.

Darling, what's the matter?

Venetia I've got a headache, that's all.

Asquith Oh my darling, you must be ill, whatever the doctor says.

Venetia No, it's not that –

Asquith Oh, I hope you haven't caught something in that dreadful hospital. You must see my doctor immediately.

Venetia No, look, there's something I have to tell you.

Asquith looks concerned.

Asquith What?

Venetia takes a deep breath.

Venetia I'm getting married.

Asquith is stunned.

Asquith What?

Venetia To Edwin.

For a moment he literally can't speak.

Asquith No . . . I mean, you can't. It's impossible.

Venetia I'm sorry, but I always told you I'd get married one day.

Asquith Yes, but not now. And not him!

Venetia looks at him.

Venetia Why not?

Asquith Well . . . it's obvious. It's a joke. We've always laughed at such an idea.

Venetia But why?

Asquith Well . . . I'm fond of him, as you know, and recognise his merits, but . . .

Venetia Yes?

Asquith Well, he's not a man. Just a bundle of moods and nerves and symptoms, intensely self-absorbed, and – well, I won't go on.

Venetia Jewish?

Asquith . . . I can't say that is irrelevant. And no one can accuse me of being an anti-Semite, the first Prime Minister ever to appoint Jews to his Cabinet.

Venetia No . . . you've made him what he is. He knows that.

Asquith And this is how he repays me.

Beat.

And what about his father's will? Everyone knows he has to marry a Jewess or he'll lose his inheritance. So you'd be left penniless.

Venetia No, we won't.

Asquith What?

Venetia hesitates.

Venetia I'm going to convert.

Asquith is horrified.

Asquith Oh Venetia . . . How could you?

Venetia says nothing.

I mean, to turn your back on Christianity, the main force which has created the West – has remoulded and transformed the world, and made us what we are – and adopt in its place that narrow, sterile, tribal creed . . . To declare that Christ was no more than a fantasist, a liar, an impostor. How can you think of it?

Venetia hesitates.

Just for the money?

Venetia No, not just. It will make me acceptable to his family too.

Pause.

Asquith When did you decide this? Just now, when I was out of the room?

Venetia No. About a month ago.

Asquith is stunned.

I know. I should have told you earlier, but it never seemed like the right moment.

Asquith And now is?

Venetia I couldn't wait any longer. The wedding's set for next month.

Asquith And the conversion?

Venetia Next week.

Pause.

Asquith Look, there's still time to think again.

Venetia I have. He first asked me three years ago, after that holiday in Sicily . . . My mind is made up, though. I'm going through with it.

Asquith takes it in.

Asquith And you can honestly say you love him?

Venetia hesitates.

Venetia I'm very fond of him. And I think we'll be happy together.

Asquith How could you be, when you've sacrificed your faith?

Venetia I have no faith.

Asquith is shocked.

To me it's just a label. And one label's as good as another as far as I'm concerned.

She goes.
Asquith is left alone.

SIX

The same. A few days later.
Asquith stands at the window looking out.
Montagu enters.

Montagu You wanted to see me?

Asquith Yes. Come in. Please.

Montagu Thank you.

Montagu shuts the door and moves further into the room.
Pause.

Asquith Just tell me, has she done it yet?

Montagu What?

Asquith Has she become a Jew?

Montagu Yes.

Asquith flinches in pain.

Asquith How could you make her go through with it?

Montagu I didn't make her.

Asquith You wouldn't have married her otherwise?

Montagu says nothing.
Asquith smiles grimly.

Montagu Look, I'm sorry if we've hurt you.

Asquith Well, you needn't be, because I don't care a damn about me, or you indeed. All I care about is her happiness.

Montagu Well, I'll do my best.

Asquith (*sceptically*) Hm . . .

He composes himself.

Anyway, that isn't why I sent for you.

Montagu It isn't?

Asquith No.

He picks up a newspaper on his desk.

As you will have seen in *The Times* today, Northcliffe and his crew are still blaming the failure of our attacks on the Western Front on a shortage of shells.

Montagu Yes . . .

Asquith And now Admiral Fisher's resigned over this Dardanelles business.

Montagu So I heard.

Asquith Well, having consulted with Lloyd George and Balfour, I've decided that for the sake of national unity, I must disband the Government and form a coalition.

Montagu is stunned.

Montagu A coalition?

Asquith Yes. I'm replacing Churchill with Balfour at the Admiralty, bringing Curzon in as Lord Privy Seal and putting Lloyd George in charge of munitions.

Montagu But that's suicide . . .

Asquith Is it?

Montagu Yes. Once you let them in, they'll take over. It'll be the beginning of the end for you. Whereas if you'd just wait and see . . . Perhaps Italy will come in and –

Asquith It's too late to wait and see. I've already seen the King.

Montagu is appalled.

Anyway, how it affects you is that . . . well, with the Tories coming in, obviously others will have to make way for them . . .

Montagu takes this in.

Montagu You're sacking me?

Asquith . . . I wouldn't put it like that. But I am suspending your Cabinet rank.

Beat.

You can, of course, return to your old job at the Treasury.

Pause.

Montagu (*getting up*) Well, if that's all . . .

He goes to the door.

Asquith Edwin . . .

Montagu stops.

Look, I want you to know . . . this has nothing to do with Venetia. It's a purely . . . political matter. You know that, don't you?

Montagu hesitates.

Montagu Of course.

Montagu goes, leaving Asquith alone with his misery.
Asquith opens a drawer in his desk and takes out a photograph of Venetia.
He looks at it for a moment.
Then quickly puts it back again before walking off.

SEVEN

The house of Lord Swaythling (Montagu's brother), 28 Kensington Court.
A chupah (a white Jewish wedding canopy supported by four poles) stands on the stage.
Rabbi Joseph, in full ceremonial dress, stands facing the audience with Montagu, stage right, in tails and yarmulke (skullcap), and Venetia, stage left, wearing a veil and a stunning white wedding gown.

Rabbi Joseph Do you, Edwin Samuel Montagu, take Beatrice Venetia Stanley to be your wife, to love, to honour and to cherish her as a faithful husband?

Montagu I do.

Rabbi Joseph turns to Venetia.

Rabbi Joseph Do you, Beatrice Venetia Stanley, take Edwin Samuel Montagu to be your husband, to love, to honour and to cherish him as a faithful wife?

Venetia I do.

Rabbi Joseph smiles and passes Montagu a silver goblet full of red wine. As Rabbi Joseph speaks, Montagu drinks from the goblet, then passes it to Venetia, who also drinks from it.

Rabbi Joseph Blessed art thou, O Lord our God, King of the Universe, who hast created the fruit of the vine, symbol of joy. Blessed art thou, Our Lord, who hast hallowed thy people by the blessing of the marriage canopy and the sacred covenant of marriage.

Venetia gives the goblet back to Rabbi Joseph.
Montagu places a ring on Venetia's right forefinger.

Montagu By this ring you are consecrated to me according to the law of Moses and Israel.

Venetia By this ring you are consecrated to me according to the law of Moses and Israel.

Rabbi Joseph You are now husband and wife according to the law of Moses and Israel.

Rabbi Joseph picks up a glass, wraps it in a white napkin and places it on the ground next to Montagu.
Montagu stamps on it, smashing the glass.
Then turns to Venetia, lifts her veil and kisses her passionately on the lips.
The lights fade.

Act Two

ONE

Two years later, 1917.
The drawing room of the Montagus' house.
Early evening.
Venetia is seated with a drink.
Montagu walks around the room with a glass of Scotch in his hand.
Pause.

Venetia You're sure he said seven?

Montagu Yes.

She looks at her watch.

Venetia It's half-past.

Montagu I know.

Beat.

Venetia Perhaps he won't come?

Montagu Of course he'll come. He specifically wants to meet you.

Venetia He said that?

Montagu Yes. He wants to ask you a favour.

Venetia looks puzzled.

Venetia But I don't see what conceivable favour I could do a man like Beaverbrook.

Montagu Neither do I, but he's a very influential man, so if you can conceivably see your way to accommodating him, I should be very grateful . . . Within reason, of course.

Pause.

Venetia And you really think this could help your career?

Montagu Of course. Lloyd George only got into power because of the backing of Beaverbrook's newspapers, so he's entirely indebted to him.

Venetia The new Northcliffe . . .

Montagu Yes. But even more powerful.

He reflects and clenches his fist in frustration.

And I must get back into the Cabinet . . . I'm sick of fiddling with figures at the Treasury. I want to be back at the heart of things, like I used to be.

Venetia I know. And I want you to be too. So don't worry. I'm sure I can play 'the good wife' . . . in this way at least.

They exchange a meaningful glance.
Pause.
The doorbell goes.
They look at each other again.
Then Montagu goes out.
Beaverbrook speaks with a Canadian accent.

Beaverbrook (*off*) Ah, Edwin, sorry I'm late. I got held up at the paper.

Montagu (*off*) Not at all. Do come in.

Beaverbrook (*off*) Thank you.

Montagu comes in with Beaverbrook, thirty-eight, stockily built and attractive.
Beaverbrook and Venetia take each other in.

Montagu Venetia, this is Max Beaverbrook. Max, my wife.

Venetia How do you do.

Beaverbrook I am delighted to meet you, Mrs Montagu.

They shake hands.
Beaverbrook holds on to her hand a moment longer than necessary and smiles.
Montagu sees this and hesitates for a moment.
Finally, Beaverbrook lets go of her hand.

Montagu My dear . . . Did I tell you that as well as being Canada's official representative here, Max has just added the *Daily Express* to his portfolio of newspapers?

Venetia Really? Then I must buy it one day.

Beaverbrook Well, millions do. But from what I hear, you don't need to read newspapers.

Venetia How do you mean?

Beaverbrook They say you're the most well-informed woman in London.

She smiles.

Venetia Yes, well . . . not any more.

Beaverbrook Oh. What a pity . . .

He looks at her.
Pause.

Montagu Well, Max, what can I get you to drink?

Beaverbrook Scotch, please.

Montagu Right.

Montagu goes to the drinks table.

Venetia Do sit down, Lord Beaverbrook.

Beaverbrook Oh, please, call me Max. I haven't got used to the title yet.

Venetia Very well. Max.

Beaverbrook Thank you. I will.

He sits down.

But I mustn't stay long. I'm due for dinner at Number Ten.

Venetia and Montagu glance at each other.
Montagu brings him a drink.

Montagu Your Scotch.

Beaverbrook Thank you.

He takes his drink and he and Montagu sit down.
Pause as Beaverbrook drinks.
Montagu and Venetia then take a sip too.
Beaverbrook looks at Venetia and smiles.

So, Mrs Montagu, I don't know if Edwin told you, but I've been wanting to meet you for some time.

Venetia Yes, actually, he did. And I'm most flattered.

Beaverbrook smiles.

Beaverbrook Good . . . Well, I'll come straight to the point then.

He looks at her.

I'm collecting material for a book I want to write when the war's over and I thought maybe you could help me.

Venetia Me?

Beaverbrook Yes.

Venetia How?

Beaverbrook Well . . . it's well known, if you don't mind my saying, that before the Coalition, you were closer to Asquith than anyone.

Venetia is taken aback.

Venetia Is it?

Beaverbrook Yes. And that in particular he used to write to you all the time, even during Cabinet.

Venetia looks at Montagu.

Venetia You are remarkably well informed.

Beaverbrook I like to be. Now, I hope you'll forgive me for being so direct, Mrs Montagu, but what it comes down to is this.

He looks at her.

I'd like to see those letters.

Pause.
Venetia takes it in.

Venetia Let me get this absolutely clear. You, a man I've only just met, want to see my most intimate correspondence?

Beaverbrook Yes. And I'll tell you why I think you should let me.

He thinks.

This war . . . this terrible, terrible war . . . has been about the worst thing that's ever happened to this country, right? Countless thousands of men have been killed or wounded. A whole generation almost wiped out . . . Your generation . . . Well, one day, I think we need to know why . . . And I'm not talking about the details of the military campaigns and the generals' tactics and so forth. I'll leave that to the academics. No, I want to write about the people back home taking the really big decisions – the politicians I mean, and the Prime Minister in particular. I want to show the kinds of pressures they're under when they take those decisions – or fail to – and what that feels like from the inside – without it being one of those self-serving memoirs. I want us to really get to know the characters of our leaders and then see the impact that has on history. Do you follow?

Venetia Yes, I think so.

Beaverbrook Good. Well, that's where you come in. Or rather, those letters.

Pause.

Venetia But what about the fact that they were written to me in confidence?

Beaverbrook Yes, well, I understand that. But on matters as important as these, surely that can't be the only consideration? Given all the thousands that have died, all those friends and relations and loved ones we've lost, don't you think the public has a right to know why?

Pause.

Of course, I'm not interested in anything of a purely personal nature, and as a newspaper man, I know how to protect my sources. But this is a story that needs to be told. Long after the war is over, of course. But not too long, or we'll all be dead. And it will be told more accurately, more truthfully, if you let me see those letters.

Venetia thinks.
Pause.

Look, I'm not expecting you to make a decision now. I don't even think you should. Take some time to think it over . . . But if there's anything you want to discuss, just let me know and we can do it over lunch. If your husband doesn't mind, that is.

Montagu On the contrary . . .

Beaverbrook looks at Venetia.

Beaverbrook And needless to say, if there's ever anything I can do for you – either of you – I'd be delighted.

Montagu Well, that's very kind of you.

Venetia Yes . . .

Beaverbrook Not at all.

He gets up.

Well, I really mustn't keep the Prime Minister waiting any longer, so I'd better . . .

Montagu (*rising*) Of course.

They get up.

Beaverbrook Well, goodbye, Mrs Montagu.

He holds his hand out and she gets up to take it.

Venetia Yes, goodbye.

He holds her hand.

Beaverbrook I'll wait to hear from you then. And thank you for listening to me.

He lets go of her hand.
Then turns to Montagu and begins to go out.

And thank you, Edwin, for introducing me to your charming wife.

Montagu It's been a pleasure.

Montagu shows him out.
Venetia remains alone on stage, looking troubled.

Montagu (*off*) Give my regards to the Prime Minister.

Beaverbrook (*off*) I'll do that. Goodnight.

Montagu (*off*) Goodnight.

The sound of the front door closing.
Montagu comes back in.
He looks at Venetia.

Montagu So . . . what do you think?

Pause.

Venetia Well, no one can say he doesn't have cheek.

Montagu Of course. That's how he got where he is today.

Beat.

Will you help him though?

Pause.
Venetia is torn.

Venetia They're private letters . . .

Montagu Yes . . . but they're also historical documents of the first importance.

Pause.

Venetia But it's so recent . . . the war isn't even over.

Montagu He promises he won't publish till years after.

Pause.

Venetia I was his closest confidante for three years . . . Don't I owe him something?

Montagu No. He stole three years of your youth, did everything he could to stop us marrying, and when we did, terminated my Cabinet career.

He looks at her.

And Beaverbrook could get it back . . .

She looks at him.
The lights fade.

TWO

Balfour, wearing pince-nez, is working at his desk at the Foreign Office.

There is a knock at the door.

Balfour Come in.

The door opens and Weizmann enters, carrying a briefcase.

Ah, Dr Weizmann. Good to see you again. Please, come and sit down.

Weizmann Thank you.

Weizmann closes the door and sits down.

Balfour How's Manchester?

Weizmann Manchester? I'm not sure. You see, I've moved to London.

Balfour Oh, I didn't know. Whereabouts?

Weizmann Kensington. It is more convenient for my work. My war work, I mean.

Balfour Oh yes, of course. Now, I wanted to thank you for that. Your invention has made a real difference to our shell production and you will be justly compensated for it in due course.

Weizmann Yes, well, as I've said to the Prime Minister, that can wait till after the war.

Balfour Well, it's most understanding of you. And I know the Prime Minister appreciates it too.

They smile.

Anyway, what can I do for you?

Weizmann Well, when we last met two years ago, you kindly said I might come and see you again when there was something you could do for me.

Balfour Yes . . . ?

Weizmann Well, I had assumed that would be when the war was over, but for a number of reasons, I find that time is actually, well, now.

He smiles.

Balfour Indeed?

Weizmann Yes. You see, I have heard a rumour, but a reliable rumour, that northern Palestine has been promised to the French . . .

Balfour (*disingenuously*) Really?

Weizmann Yes – they see it apparently as merely southern Syria. And there has of course long been a rumour, also reliable, that Palestine may be included in the lands promised to the Sharif of Mecca as a reward for rising up, with the help of Colonel Lawrence, against the Turks.

Balfour Mm . . .

He thinks.

Well, as Foreign Secretary, I can assure you that with regard to the future of Palestine, nothing has been finally decided yet and that I personally am still very sympathetic to your cause. As, I know, is the Prime Minister.

Weizmann That is good to hear.

Weizmann takes a copy of The Times *out of his briefcase.*

But then there is also this letter in today's *Times*. Have you seen it?

He offers it to him, open at the letters page.

Balfour No, I tend not to read the newspapers.

Weizmann (*surprised*) Really? You don't think you might occasionally learn something?

Balfour Perhaps. But I have never put myself to the trouble of rummaging an immense rubbish heap on the problematical chance of discovering a cigar end.

Weizmann smiles.

Weizmann Well, you're right about this. It is definitely part of the rubbish. It is an anti-Zionist tirade from, believe it or not, the Presidents of the Anglo-Jewish Association and the Board of Deputies of British Jews clearly intended to influence the Government against us.

Balfour Well, they've failed to influence me.

Weizmann I'm glad to hear it. But what about your colleagues?

Balfour Ah well, I cannot speak for them.

Weizmann Exactly. And that is why I am here. I and my colleagues at the Zionist Organisation think now is the moment for some kind of public statement of the Government's sympathy with our aims. Some kind of announcement . . . or declaration, if you like, of your support.

Balfour I see.

Weizmann And now General Allenby is by all accounts making such good progress, we can be confident we are no longer in the world of the hypothetical, can we not?

Balfour Oh, certainly. The Prime Minister wants Jerusalem by Christmas.

Weizmann Excellent.

They smile.
Balfour thinks.

Balfour So, what is it you wish the Government to back? A Jewish state at the end of the war?

Weizmann No, we are not ready for that. The Arabs already outnumbered the Jews in Palestine by six to one at the start of the war and many of our people have left since then, so we cannot hope to set up a Jewish state yet. No, we must begin with what we would like to call a National Home for the Jewish people under British protection.

Balfour A 'National Home'?

Weizmann Yes, it is a phrase taken from the first Zionist Congress held in Basel twenty years ago.

Balfour And what exactly does it mean?

Weizmann It means, or will come to mean, a Jewish state – after all, what is a nation but a state? – but it has a better chance of not immediately antagonising the Arabs, as in the meantime it can mean something less. If you follow.

Balfour (*admiringly*) Yes . . . clever.

Weizmann (*quickly*) Though of course, a home is exactly what the Jewish people do want and need.

Balfour thinks it over.

Balfour Very well. Draft something along the lines you want and I'll take a look at it before presenting it to my colleagues.

Weizmann I'm much obliged to you. And you won't regret it. You will have the eternal gratitude of the Jewish people for this.

Balfour Yes, well, I can't promise anything. It will have to go before the Cabinet. But it obviously helps that the Prime Minister is sympathetic.

Weizmann I hope so. And thank you again. Ah, if only Mr Samuel was still in office too . . .

Balfour Yes . . .

Weizmann gets up.

Oh, that reminds me. I should warn you. There is one problem . . .

Weizmann What?

Balfour Edwin Montagu is back in the Cabinet.

Weizmann is surprised.

It's being announced today. Secretary of State for India.

Weizmann looks concerned.
The lights fade.

THREE

The drawing room of the Montagus' house by lamplight.
Venetia enters wearing a stole over a glamorous low-cut evening dress. Her diamond earrings and necklace sparkle in the lamplight.
A man in black tie comes into the room after her. But it's not Montagu. It's Beaverbrook.
She turns round and faces him.
She seems a little nervous. He, confident.

Venetia He's not back yet.

Beaverbrook Oh.

Beat.

Venetia The debate must still be going on.

Beaverbrook Yes, well, that's the trouble with these politicians. They never stop talking.

She smiles.

Except Edwin, of course.

Venetia Of course.

They smile.

Venetia Anyway, thank you for a lovely evening.

Beaverbrook It's been a pleasure. As always. And most helpful for my book. We must do it again soon.

Venetia Yes, well . . . if there's anything else in the letters you want me to explain, just –

Beaverbrook I will.

They smile and look at each other.
Pause.

Well, I'd better –

Venetia Look, I'm sure he'll be back soon, so why don't you stay and have a drink?

She indicates the drinks table.
He looks at her, surprised.
Then smiles.

Beaverbrook Thanks. I'd like that. And you'll have one?

Venetia Why not?

He nods and goes over to the drinks table. Then begins making the drinks.

Venetia takes her stole off and throws it over the back of the sofa.

Beaverbrook I guess Edwin's been working pretty hard now he's back in the Cabinet.

Venetia Yes. All the time really.

Beaverbrook The new boy wants to impress, huh?

Venetia Mm . . .

He gives her a glass and they drink.

Beaverbrook Well, maybe I can help with that.

Venetia You already have. He's most appreciative of what your paper's been saying about him.

Beaverbrook And about his wife, I hope.

He indicates a headline with his hands.

'The Beautiful Mrs Montagu'.

She smiles, flattered.
Pause.
They look at each other.
Then he moves towards her and kisses her.
Finally, he steps back.

Sorry.

She thinks.

Venetia No . . . it's all right.

He smiles.
Then she moves towards him and they kiss again, this time more passionately.
The sound of the front door closing, off.
They stop and Venetia looks concerned.

Beaverbrook Ah. That must be him.

Venetia Yes.

Beaverbrook drinks.

So does she, trying to look relaxed.
Shortly, Montagu enters, looking tired.

Beaverbrook Hello, Edwin.

Montagu (*surprised*) Oh . . . Max. Hello.

He looks at Venetia.

Beaverbrook How was the debate?

Montagu Exhausting, but we won.

Beaverbrook Good.

An awkward pause.

Well, I look forward to seeing what our reporter made of it. And whatever he made of it, I'll make it better.

Montagu smiles.

Now, I must go and put the paper to bed.

Montagu Yes, well, thank you for looking after Venetia for me.

Beaverbrook Not at all.

Montagu I hope you got what you wanted.

Beaverbrook glances at Venetia.

Beaverbrook Yes.

Montagu Good.

Beaverbrook smiles.

Beaverbrook Well, goodnight.

Montagu Goodnight.

He smiles at Venetia, who nods back at him.
Then goes.
They wait until the sound of the front door closing.

Venetia Well, I'm going to put myself to bed.

She moves towards the door.

Montagu No, wait a minute, please. I need to talk to you.

He goes over to the drinks table and pours himself a drink.
Venetia stops and waits nervously.

I've just heard some terrible news.

Venetia is surprised.

There's a plan afoot at the Foreign Office to make a Declaration in favour of the Zionists.

Venetia is relieved.

Venetia Oh . . .

Montagu It's coming before the Cabinet tomorrow and I've only just been told about it. They've been hiding it from me . . .

He drinks bitterly.
Venetia regains her composure.

Venetia . . . But I thought you'd dealt with that years ago?

Montagu So did I . . . But it's back. And this time Balfour's behind it.

Venetia looks puzzled.

Venetia Balfour?

Montagu Yes.

She thinks.

Venetia But why should he care about the Jews?

Montagu God knows. It's hard to know what goes on in that man's mind . . . Perhaps he just wants to get rid of us?

Pause.

Venetia Well, you blocked it before . . . perhaps you can again?

Montagu Perhaps. But then I had the PM on my side.

Venetia And Lloyd George isn't?

Montagu No. He made that perfectly clear last time. Anything to keep the French out of the Holy Land.

Venetia Well, what about the others?

Montagu Besides Balfour, only Milner and Curzon will be there. And Milner's the PM's man.

Venetia And Curzon?

Montagu I'm not sure. On the one hand, he's a Tory . . . but on the other, he's never forgiven Balfour for forcing him to resign as Viceroy of India when he was PM.

Venetia Well then. Perhaps he'll support you?

Montagu Perhaps. But that's still only two against three. And with the PM against me . . .

Pause.

Oh well, I suppose I only have myself to blame.

Venetia doesn't understand.

Venetia What?

Montagu If I hadn't taken you away from him, Asquith would never have let Lloyd George take over the Government in the first place.

Venetia We don't know that.

Montagu Don't we?

He looks at her.

He was never the same after he lost you.

Pause.

And he would never have countenanced this nonsense. He never took Zionism seriously for a moment.

Venetia So you regret marrying me, do you?

Montagu No, of course not. You know I don't. But I suppose every pleasure has its price . . .

Pause.
Venetia thinks.

Venetia Perhaps . . .

Montagu Yes?

Venetia Well, perhaps you should speak to Max.

Montagu Max?

Venetia Yes. You know how much influence he has with the PM . . .

Montagu thinks.

Montagu Hm . . . But not in this matter, I fear.

He finishes his drink.

Anyway, I must get to work.

Venetia is surprised.

Venetia Now?

Montagu Yes. I'm going to write a memorandum and explain to my colleagues that being Jewish is simply a matter of religion – not of race or nationality or anything else – and therefore, it should just take its place among the other religions and not seek to have its own state.

She thinks.

Venetia But you're not religious?

Montagu No.

Venetia And yet you're Jewish, aren't you?

Montagu Yes.

Venetia Well then, it can't be just a matter of religion, can it?

Montagu (*reluctantly*) No. Not yet. But I want it to be.

He looks at her.

They talk about making Palestine a 'home' for the Jewish people. But the only home I want is here with you.

He goes over and takes her hands.
Venetia looks uncomfortable.

Venetia I thought you were going to write your memorandum.

Montagu . . . You're right. I must try and stop this madness before it's too late.

He goes out.
Venetia reflects for a moment.
Then picks up her stole and goes.

FOUR

The Cabinet Room.

Lloyd George, Balfour, Montagu and Lord Curzon, a proud and arrogant man of fifty-eight, sit round the table listening as the lights come up on Milner speaking and holding up a newspaper clipping.

Milner And as if that wasn't enough, today's copy of the *Daily Mail* states that twenty thousand well-drilled men were marching about County Clare in procession, saying, 'Up, rebels, up with the Kaiser!'

Curzon Bloody traitors.

Balfour Yes, can we really allow that to happen?

Lloyd George Send a copy to the Chief Secretary for Ireland and ask him to investigate and make a report.

Milner Yes, Prime Minister.

Lloyd George looks through his papers.

Lloyd George Now, the next item on the agenda. Ah yes, the Jews . . . Mr Montagu, you would like to express a view about Mr Balfour's proposed Declaration?

Montagu Yes. Thank you, Prime Minister.

He turns to the others.

I trust you all have a copy of my memorandum, 'The Anti-Semitism of the Present Government'.

Mutters of embarrassed affirmation.

Good . . . Now, you may think that a provocative title and I stress that I am not accusing the Government of deliberate anti-Semitism, but, as the one Jewish minister in the Cabinet, I wish to place on record my view, which I hold very strongly, that the proposed Declaration would be anti-Semitic in result and would prove a rallying ground for anti-Semites in every country in the world, including Britain. For if Palestine is reconstituted as a national home for the Jews, as Mr Balfour proposes, surely it follows that the impetus to deprive the Jew of the rights of citizenship in the country in which he resides must be enormously increased. Why should the Russian, Romanian or Pole give the Jew equal rights if his national home is Palestine?

Pause.

Moreover, I deny that Palestine is today particularly associated with the Jews or properly to be regarded as a fit place for them to live. It is quite true that Palestine plays a large part in Jewish history, but so it does in Mohammedan history – the Prophet himself is said to have ascended to Heaven from the great rock in the Temple of Omar in Jerusalem – and surely it plays a larger part than any other place in Christian history. The Temple may have been in Palestine, but so was the Sermon on the Mount and the Crucifixion. I would not deny to Jews in Palestine equal rights to colonisation with those who profess other religions, but a religious test of citizenship seems to me to be tolerable only to those who take a bigoted and narrow view of one particular epoch of the history of Palestine, and to claim for the Jews a position to which they are not entitled.

Beat.

And as for the claim that the Jews are a 'nation', albeit one without a territory, it is no more true to say that a Jewish Englishman and a Jewish Moor are of the same nation than it is to say that a Christian Englishman and a Christian Frenchman are of the same nation. Of the same religion of course. Of the same race, perhaps, traced back through the centuries. But the Prime Minister and the French Prime Minister, Monsieur Briand, are, I suppose, related through the ages, one as a Welshman and the other as a Breton, but they certainly do not belong to the same nation!

Laughter.

With regard to the situation in Britain, it has been claimed that this policy would be popular with Jews and non-Jews alike. As for the general public, I have always recognised the unpopularity of my community, much greater than some people may think, and I can readily understand that many non-Jews may want to get rid of us. (*He glances at Balfour.*) Certainly we have obtained a far greater share of this country's wealth and opportunities than our numbers alone would justify, added to which, some of us have shown exclusivity in our friendships and intolerance in our attitudes. But just as there is no community of thought and mode of life among Christian Englishmen, so there is not among Jewish Englishmen. Indeed, I'm glad to think that the prejudice against intermarriage, for example, is finally breaking down, whilst more and more of our children are being educated in the same schools and universities as their Christian compatriots and going on to take part in the Army, Civil Service and, if I may say so, politics of our country.

Beat.

In conclusion, I claim that the lives that British Jews have led, the aims that they have had before them, and the part they have played in our public life and institutions have entitled them to be regarded, not as British Jews, but as Jewish Britons. And in formulating policy with regard to Jews, it is to these Jewish Britons that, I submit, the Cabinet owes its first duty. It is not, with respect, our business to espouse the cause of Zionists of largely foreign origin, naturalised though some of them may be, in the teeth of the ardent wishes of those whose families have lived for generations in this country, and who feel themselves to be Englishmen.

Lloyd George smiles.

Lloyd George Yes, well, your cousin clearly sees things differently.

Montagu cannot deny it.

However, Mr Balfour?

Balfour Thank you, Prime Minister.

He thinks.

Gentlemen, what is at the heart of the Zionist movement is the intense national consciousness held by certain members of the Jewish race. They regard themselves as one of the great historic races of the world, whose original home was Palestine, and they have a passionate longing to regain once more this ancient national home. As the Secretary of State for India says, other Jews have become absorbed into the nations among whom they and their forefathers have dwelt for many generations, and they will remain nationals of those nations. Thus, I see nothing inconsistent between the establishment of a Jewish national focus in Palestine and the complete assimilation and absorption of Jews into the nationality of other countries. Indeed, Zionism will actually help this process as once those Jews have been given a choice and chosen to remain where they are, any suspicion of a double allegiance or non-national outlook will be eliminated. Just as English emigrants to the United States become, either in the first or subsequent generations, American nationals, so, in future, if a Jewish citizenship were to be established in Palestine, would Jews become either Englishmen, Americans, Germans, or Palestinians.

He pauses.

As to the meaning of the words 'national home', to which the Zionists attach so much importance, I understand it to mean some form of British, or other protectorate, under which full facilities would be given to the Jews to work out their own salvation and to build up by means of education, agriculture, and industry, a real centre of national culture and focus of national life. It does not necessarily involve the early establishment of an independent Jewish state, which is a matter for gradual development in accordance with the ordinary laws of political evolution.

He smiles.

Lloyd George Yes, well, as a Welshman, I sympathise with the aspirations of small nationalities . . . But Lord Curzon, you would like to say something?

Curzon Yes. Mr Montagu may be the only Jewish member of the Cabinet, but I am the only member, I believe, who has actually been to Palestine and as such I would like to make some points of a practical nature.

Montagu looks hopeful.

From my recollection, Palestine, contrary to its biblical description as a land 'flowing with milk and honey', is, for the most part, a barren and desolate place. Cultivation is sparse, the valleys and streams few, large centres of population scarce – a less propitious seat for the future Jewish race can hardly be imagined.

Montagu is delighted.

Further, let it be borne in mind when we speak of this impoverished country as a 'national home' for a great people, that malaria, fever, ophthalmia, and other ailments abound, not to be eradicated save by great outlay over a long period. Such is the country – which even after patient toil from a people inured to agriculture would only be able to support a relatively small population – that we are invited, if we can get hold of it, to convert into a home for a people numbering many millions, brought from other and different climates, and to a large extent trained in other industries and professions.

He smiles.

There arises the further question of what is to become of the people of this country, assuming the Turk to be expelled. Since besides the eighty thousand or so Jews, there are, I believe, over half a million Syrian Arabs – a mixed community of Arab, Hebrew, Canaanite, Greek, Egyptian, and possibly even Crusaders' blood. They and their forefathers have occupied the country for the best part of fifteen hundred years. They own the soil, which belongs either to individual landowners or to village communities. They profess the Mohammedan faith. They will not be content either to be expropriated for Jewish immigrants, or to act merely as 'hewers of wood and drawers of water' for them. In which case, how is it proposed to get rid of this existing majority of Musulman inhabitants and introduce the Jews in their place?

He looks challengingly at Balfour.

Thus, it seems to me that this Declaration is a poisoned chalice and to secure for the Jews already in Palestine equal civil and religious rights would be a far better aim than to attempt repatriation on a large scale. I regard the latter as sentimental idealism, which will never be realised, and His Majesty's Government should have nothing to do with it.

Lloyd George looks to Balfour.

Balfour So far as the Arabs generally are concerned, I hope they will remember that it is Great Britain that is fighting to free them from the tyranny of their brutal conqueror, who has kept them under his heel for so many centuries, and that therefore they will not grudge that small notch in what are now Arab territories being given to the people who for yet more centuries have been separated from it.

He pauses for a moment.

As for the natives of Palestine, Zionism – be it right or wrong, good or bad – is rooted in age-long traditions, present needs and future hopes, of far profounder import than the desires and prejudices of the seven hundred thousand Arabs who now inhabit that ancient land.

Curzon looks sceptical.

Lloyd George Mm . . . what about the French, though?

Balfour Well, it so happens, I have here a recent letter from Monsieur Jules Cambon of the French Foreign Ministry to Mr Nahum Sokolow of the World Zionist Organisation, which provides some guidance. It reads, in translation, 'The French Government, which entered this present war to defend a people wrongly attacked, and which continues the struggle to assure the victory of right over might, can but feel sympathy for your cause, the triumph of which is bound up with that of the Allies.' So I don't think we'll have any trouble from them.

He passes it around among his colleagues.

Lloyd George How about the Americans? And the Russians?

Balfour Well, I confess that so far the messages from the President have been somewhat mixed. And as for the Russians, events are moving so quickly there, one hardly knows who to ask. What I can say though is that the vast majority of Jews in both Russia and America – as indeed, all over the world – are in favour of Zionism, notwithstanding the opposition of a number of wealthy Jews here.

He glances at Montagu.

So from a purely political point of view, this Declaration would allow us to carry on some extremely useful propaganda in those countries.

Lloyd George Mm . . .

Balfour Finally, I would like to draw the Cabinet's attention to the fact that the German Government are at this very moment making great efforts to capture the support of the Zionist movement and may be preparing their own Declaration. I have here a translation of a recent article from *Der Reichsbote* which Dr Weizmann has passed on to me and there have been many similar articles in other German newspapers.

He passes round the article.

So there is a real danger that if we don't, they will.

Curzon glances at the article before passing it on.

Curzon Yes, well, I do not deny that there may be purely propaganda reasons, though no others, for expressing a degree of sympathy with the Zionist movement. However, we should at least consider whether in the long term we are encouraging a practical ideal, or merely preparing the way for disappointment and failure.

Balfour hesitates for a moment.

Balfour The Lord President of the Council is right. I do not deny that this is an adventure. And it may fail . . . But are we never to have adventures? Are we never to try new experiments?

Montagu Not this one, I beg you.

No one speaks for a moment.
Milner finishes writing something he's been quietly working away at.

Milner If I may, Prime Minister?

Lloyd George Yes.

Milner Well, to take account of Mr Montagu and Lord Curzon's concerns, I would like to propose the following alternative draft Declaration.

Lloyd George Go on.

He reads from a scrap of paper he's been writing on.

Milner 'His Majesty's Government view with favour the establishment *in* Palestine of a national home for the Jewish people, and will use their best endeavours to facilitate the achievement of this object, *it being clearly understood that nothing shall be done which may prejudice the civil and religious rights of existing non-Jewish communities in Palestine, or the rights and political status enjoyed by Jews in any other country.*'

Balfour Excellent.

Montagu No words of qualification can prevent the evil consequences of such a Declaration. I object to any formula that states that Palestine is the 'national home' of the Jewish people, or even that there is to be a national home for the Jewish people *in* Palestine. The Jews are, or should be at least, a religious community, like any other. Not a nation.

Balfour and Milner shrug.

Lloyd George Well, since we cannot agree, I suggest we show that to President Wilson and see what he says.

Milner Very good.

Montagu looks concerned, Curzon aloof.
Balfour looks content.

Lloyd George Now, what next?

The lights begin to fade as Milner finds the next item on the agenda.

Milner The War Aims Committee has run out of money.

Lloyd George Ah . . .

The lights fade to black.

FIVE

The Montagus' home.
Venetia is looking at some architect's plans.
A phone rings offstage.
She ignores it.
It stops ringing.

Montagu (*off*) Hello? . . . Speaking . . . (*Pause.*) I see . . . Thank you for letting me know.

Pause.
Shortly, Montagu comes in, wearing a long black coat.
Venetia looks up at him.

Montagu Well, the Declaration is to be made. The President has agreed.

She puts the plans aside.

Venetia I'm sorry.

Montagu Yes, so am I.

He reflects.

It seems strange to be a member of a Government which goes out of its way to deal this blow at a colleague who is doing his best to be loyal to them . . . They are dealing an irreparable blow to Jewish Britons, alarming the whole Muslim world and endeavouring to set up a people which does not exist . . . And why we should intern people in India for Pan-Islamism when we encourage Pan-Judaism, I cannot for the life of me understand.

Pause.

Venetia Cousin Herbert will be pleased . . .

Montagu Yes . . .

Pause.

Anyway, I should be going.

Venetia Already?

Montagu Well, I don't want to miss the boat, do I?

Venetia No. I suppose not.

He hesitates for a moment.

Montagu I wish you were coming with me.

Venetia I know. So do I. I've always wanted to see India. But you do understand, don't you? There's so much work to do on the new house. And you know how long we've waited to get Lutyens . . . We can't afford to put him off now.

Montagu No . . . I'm sure you're right.

Pause.

Venetia Six months isn't all that long.

Montagu tries to smile but can't.

Montagu It seems long to me.

Pause.

You're not going to be alone tonight, I hope.

Venetia No. (*A slight hesitation.*) Max is coming round.

Montagu Oh.

Venetia I've found a few more letters for him to look at . . . And after all he's done for us, well, I thought it was the least I could do to have him for supper.

Montagu Yes. Good idea.

He forces a smile.
Pause.

Look, darling, in case I don't come back –

Venetia Why wouldn't you come back?

Montagu Oh, I don't know. But with all those German submarines around –

Venetia Nonsense.

Montagu Well, you never know. It happened to Kitchener. Anyway, just in case, I want you to know . . .

Venetia Yes?

Montagu I want you to know how grateful I am to you.

Venetia can't meet his eyes.

Venetia Don't be silly.

Montagu I'm not. I mean it. My life, ever since I've known you, has been happier than it was before.

Pause.

So, while I'm away, do what you want, go where you please, whatever brings you happiness. All right? For my sake.

He kisses her.

Goodbye.

He goes.
Venetia is left alone.
The front door slams off.
Pause.
She begins to cry.
Long pause.
As the lights begin to fade, Beaverbrook enters and embraces her.
She rests her head on his shoulder as the lights fade to black.

SIX

The London Opera House, 2 December.
A spot comes up on Samuel as he stands alone at the front of the stage and speaks to the audience.

Samuel When I think of our exile, I see in my mind's eye those millions in Eastern Europe all through the centuries, crowded, cramped, proscribed, bent with oppression, suffering all the miseries of active minds denied scope, of talent not allowed to speak, of genius that cannot act . . . I see them, enduring, suffering everything, sacrificing everything in order to keep alight the flame of which they knew themselves to be the lamp, to keep alive the idea of which they knew themselves to be the vessel, to preserve the soul of which they knew themselves to be the body – their eyes always set upon one distant point, always believing that somehow, some day, the ancient greatness would be restored – always saying when they met in their families on Passover Night, 'Next year in Jerusalem . . .' Year after year, generation following generation, century succeeding century, till the time that has elapsed is counted in thousands of years, still they said, 'Next year in Jerusalem . . .'

He pauses.

If that cherished vision is at last to be realised, if on the Hills of Zion a Jewish civilisation is restored with something of its old intellectual and moral force, then among those left in the other countries of the world, I can see growing a new confidence and a new greatness. There will be a fresh light in those eyes, those bent backs will at last stand erect, there will be a greater dignity in the Jew throughout the world . . . That is why we meet today to thank the British Government – our own Government – that has made all this possible, that we shall be able to say, not as a pious and distant wish, but as a near and confident hope, '*L'shanah haba'ah b'Yerushalayim.*' 'Next year in Jerusalem.'

Loud applause.
Fade out.

SEVEN

Seven years later.
Government House, The Mount of Olives, Jerusalem, 1 April 1925.
A bowl of oranges sits on a table. Oriental rugs adorn the walls and floor.
A servant, Abdullah, stands on duty by the door.
Weizmann enters, wearing an academic robe and carrying a mortar board, and looks around.

Weizmann Where's the High Commissioner?

Abdullah Getting dressed, sir.

Weizmann And Lord Balfour?

Abdullah In his bath, sir.

Weizmann But they've had breakfast?

Abdullah Yes, sir.

Weizmann Good.

He goes to the table, puts the mortar board down, takes an orange from the bowl and begins peeling it.
He wonders what to do with the peel.
Abdullah holds out his hand.
Weizmann deposits the peel in it.

Thank you.

Abdullah continues standing to attention.

Weizmann pops a piece of orange in his mouth and wanders over to a table covered with newspapers.
He picks one up and glances at it. Then another and another.

What are these doing here?

Abdullah They are the newspapers, sir. We always have the newspapers.

Weizmann But can't you see what they're saying about Lord Balfour? And these awful black borders to illustrate, I suppose, that they are in mourning. Has he seen them yet?

Abdullah No, sir, he took breakfast in bed.

Weizmann Well, thank God for that. Take them away before he does.

Abdullah But sir, can he read Arabic?

Weizmann looks at him.

Weizmann Just take them away.

Abdullah shrugs.

Abdullah Very good, sir.

He scoops up the papers.

Weizmann You can leave that one.

Abdullah looks at him surprised.

We bribe the editor.

Abdullah gives a little smile.

Abdullah Very good, sir.

He goes out with the papers.
Weizmann picks up one of the remaining papers and begins to read.

Shortly, Samuel enters, dressed in a ceremonial white tropical uniform with a gold sash across his shoulder, a white, steel-spiked helmet and a sword by his side.

Samuel Good morning, Dr Weizmann.

Weizmann (*closing his paper*) Good morning, Sir Herbert. You look . . . most impressive, if I may say so.

Samuel Thank you. So do you.

Weizmann Ah well, a mere Doctor of Chemistry cannot compete with a High Commissioner.

Samuel smiles.

Samuel Lord Balfour not up yet?

Weizmann No. I gather he's in the bath.

Samuel Ah well. We didn't get to bed till rather late last night.

Weizmann Well, I hope we haven't worn him out too much. After all, he has been doing a lot of travelling these past few days . . . To Tel Aviv to open Balfour Street, then up to the Galilee to see the new colony of Balfouria. And to Shmuel, of course, in your honour.

Samuel smiles.

Samuel Yes . . . haven't they named something after you yet?

Weizmann No, not yet. But I am satisfied for the moment with my University.

Samuel Of course.

They smile.

So, is everything ready for the opening?

Weizmann Yes, I believe so. I've just been up there to check. (*He smiles.*) Ah, I can't wait for Lord Balfour to see it. The setting is so beautiful. Up there on Mount Scopus you can see the hills of Moab and Gilead and the spot where the children of Israel first crossed the Jordan at the end of their journey from Egypt. And today the weather is clear enough to even get a glimpse of the Dead Sea in the distance. And of course Mount Scopus was the very hill from which the Romans conducted their siege before they destroyed the city and the Temple. Yes, it is indeed the perfect site for this great symbol of Jewish renaissance.

Samuel Yes . . .

They smile.

Weizmann I just hope the Arab protest doesn't spoil it. All those horrible black flags hanging from their windows. The shops and bazaars all shut. Not to mention the newspaper articles, the speeches . . .

Samuel Yes, well, I've employed a hundred extra police so we should be all right.

Weizmann Good.

Pause.

Anyway, today is not the day to think of such things. It is a day for celebration. Speaking of which, I'd like to take this opportunity, if I may, to thank you for all you've done for us. It is ten years now since we first met in London and we have achieved a lot together since then, have we not?

Samuel (*reflecting*) Yes, we have . . .

Weizmann I'm only sorry your term as High Commissioner is coming to an end.

Samuel Thank you.

Weizmann We shall miss you.

Samuel smiles.

Samuel Yes, well, as a matter of fact . . .

Weizmann Yes?

Samuel Oh, I think I can tell you, though it isn't official yet.

Weizmann What?

Samuel Well, I'm not really going.

Weizmann You are to continue as High Commissioner?

Samuel No, but I'm staying on as a private citizen. I'm going to live on Mount Carmel and write philosophy. As I've always dreamed.

Weizmann takes this in.

Weizmann Then you are making *aliyah*?

Samuel (*struck by the idea*) Yes . . . I suppose I am really.

Weizmann That is the mark of the true Zionist.

They smile.

Samuel But what about you? Will you ever return to chemistry?

Weizmann I hope so one day, but for the moment I must devote myself to Zionism and go to America to raise money.

He looks at Samuel.

Ah well, it is hard to serve two masters, isn't it?

Samuel smiles, a little embarrassed.
Pause.

Balfour enters, wearing a black and gold gown (as the Chancellor of Cambridge University) and carrying the black and gold mortar board.

Ah, good morning, Lord Balfour.

Balfour Good morning. (*To Samuel.*) Good morning.

Samuel Good morning.

Weizmann You slept well I trust.

Balfour Like a baby. I say, Samuel, you look . . . splendid.

Samuel Thank you. So do you. But please excuse me, I must leave you, not for the first time, in the capable hands of Dr Weizmann and make sure everything is in order for our return. We have a performance of Handel's *Belshazzar* arranged for you this evening. In Hebrew.

Balfour (*uncertain*) Oh good.

Weizmann Yes and how fitting. Just as the Persian King, Cyrus, liberated the Jews from Babylon and invited them back to Jerusalem to rebuild the Temple, so you have liberated us from exile and enabled us to build the University, our modern Temple.

Samuel Indeed.

He goes out.

Balfour Well, it wasn't *just* me.

Weizmann You are too modest.

They smile.

Balfour So, Dr Weizmann, you have been looking forward to this day for some time, have you not?

Weizmann That, if I may say so, Lord Balfour, is an understatement. Today is the greatest day of my life.

Balfour Better even than the Declaration?

Weizmann Forgive me, but yes. That was merely a step on the road to fulfilment. This *is* fulfilment. Or at least, the beginning of fulfilment.

Balfour Then my journey has been worthwhile.

Weizmann . . . I am most grateful to you.

Pause.

Balfour So, this University of yours, how many undergraduates will you be taking?

Weizmann Actually, none.

Balfour None?

Weizmann For the moment. Baron Edmond de Rothschild insisted. We shall start as a research institute. But we shall soon grow. Then we will create the hundred-per-cent educated Jew to go with the hundred-per-cent Jewish labourer you have seen on our settlements.

Balfour Mm . . . And your numbers generally are increasing satisfactorily?

Weizmann Oh yes. Never better. We expect over thirty thousand this year.

Balfour (*impressed*) Really . . . And where are they coming from?

Weizmann Poland mainly, because of the government's anti-Semitic policies there, but there are signs of things happening in Germany too, what with the activities of Herr Hitler. And now America has introduced its quota system, where else is there for our people to go? So, you see, your Declaration came just in time.

He smiles.

Balfour And when might you be ready for independence?

Weizmann Well, if we can keep up our current pace, I hope for a completely Jewish Palestine in fifty years.

Balfour *Completely* Jewish?

Weizmann Yes.

Balfour But what about the Arabs?

Weizmann Sadly, despite all our efforts, the majority refuse to accept us. So . . . they will have to go elsewhere.

Balfour takes this in.
Pause.
Abdullah comes in holding a piece of paper.

Yes?

Abdullah A telegram has arrived for Lord Balfour.

Balfour Oh, thank you.

Abdullah gives it to him.
Then goes.

Excuse me.

Weizmann Of course.

Weizmann watches with concern as Balfour takes out his pince-nez, puts them on, and begins reading the telegram.
Pause.
Balfour knits his brow.

Not bad news, I hope.

Balfour No . . . But I see not everyone is as admiring of my Declaration as you . . . This is from the Muslim and Christian Association of Palestine.

Weizmann looks apprehensive.

They say that the National Home is 'a bone in the throat of the Arab world' . . . that the Declaration was made without their being consulted so they cannot accept it as deciding their destiny . . . and that I am 'the personification of Zionist injustice'.

Weizmann is appalled.

Weizmann I do apologise, Lord Balfour. You shouldn't have had to read such poison.

Balfour Not at all. I faced far worse when I was Chief Secretary for Ireland.

Weizmann is relieved.

Weizmann Well, I hope it hasn't spoilt your day.

Balfour On the contrary, I find it all so extraordinarily interesting . . .

He reflects.
Weizmann looks uncertain.
Pause.
Samuel returns.

Samuel Well, everything is in order for our return.

Weizmann Good. Then I will go and see if the car is ready.

Samuel Thank you.

Weizmann goes.
Samuel and Balfour are left alone.
Pause.

Balfour Oh, by the way . . . I just wanted to say how sorry I was about your cousin.

Samuel Oh yes . . . very sad. But he always said he'd die young.

Balfour You grew up together, didn't you?

Samuel Well, to an extent. His father was my guardian. But I was nine years older. And we were never close.

Balfour No . . .

He reflects for a moment.

And he never came here, I suppose?

Samuel smiles at the thought.

Samuel No . . . But he did write me a letter, not long before he died.

Balfour Oh yes. And had he changed his mind?

Samuel Not exactly. He said that he would have given anything for your Declaration not to have been made, but a British promise is a British promise and must be honoured.

Balfour Well, he was wrong about that. We can't keep all our promises, can we?

He smiles.

Still, nice that Venetia had a child . . .

Samuel Yes. A little girl . . . She must be about four or five now . . .

He reflects and, as he does so, a Little Girl runs on to the front of the stage in a black coat and hat. She turns and looks behind her.

Balfour Mm . . . she looked about that.

Samuel is surprised.

Samuel You've met her then?

Balfour Yes, I saw her at the funeral. (*Beat.*) Playing with Lord Beaverbrook . . .

Samuel nods.

Samuel Ah . . .

Beaverbrook, in morning dress, and Venetia, in black, walk towards the Little Girl, Beaverbrook picks her up and they go off.

Balfour Incidentally, have you read his new book, *Politicians and the War*?

Samuel No, not yet.

Balfour Oh, you must. It's absolutely fascinating . . . I'll leave it behind for you when I go.

Samuel Thank you.

They smile.
Weizmann comes back in.

Weizmann The car is waiting outside. So, if you are ready, Lord Balfour . . .

Balfour Of course. Now, have I got my speech?

He checks his pocket.

Ah, yes. Here it is. Good.

Weizmann Come then, gentlemen. Let us open the University.

Weizmann picks up his mortar board and, with deep satisfaction, ushers Samuel and Balfour out of the room.
The sound of the car doors closing and the car driving away.
Pause.
Then slowly the sound of voices becomes audible, shouting words of protest in Arabic.
The sound of the Arab protest gradually increases in anger and volume until it fills the auditorium.
Then dies away as we fade to black.

The End.